TOP 10 WORLD SERIES MVPs

Jeff C. Young

SPORTS TOP 10

Enslow Publishers, Inc.

40 Industrial Road	PO Box 38
Box 398	Aldershot
Berkeley Heights, NJ 07922	Hants GU12 6BP
USA	UK

http://www.enslow.com

Library of Congress Cataloging-in-Publication Data

Young, Jeff C., 1948–
    Top 10 World Series MVPs / Jeff C. Young
        p. cm. — (Sports top 10)
    Includes bibliographical references (p. 46) and index.
    Summary: Profiles ten of the greatest World Series Most Valuable Players in
history: Johnny Bench, Scott Brosius, Roberto Clemente, Bob Gibson, Tom
Glavine, Orel Hershiser, Reggie Jackson, Sandy Koufax, Don Larsen, and Mike
Schmidt.
    ISBN 0-7660-1497-5
    1. Baseball players—United States—Juvenile literature. 2. World Series
(Baseball)—Juvenile literature. 3. Most Valuable Player Award (Baseball)—
Juvenile literature. [1. Baseball players. 2. World Series (Baseball). 3. Most
Valuable Player Award (Baseball)] I. Title: Top 10 World Series MVPs. II. Title.
III. Series.
GV865.A1 Y66 2001
796.357'646'092273—dc21

                                                        00-008688

Printed in the United States of America

10 9 8 7 6 5 4 3 2 1

Illustration Credits: Chris Hamilton, Atlanta, Ga., pp. 11, 22, 25; National
Baseball Library & Archive, pp. 9, 14, 37, 41, 42; *The Sporting News* Archives,
pp. 13, 29, 31, 35; TRANSCENDENTAL GRAPHICS, pp. 7, 17, 18, 21, 27, 33,
38, 45.

Cover Illustration: National Baseball Library & Archive

Cover Description: Tom Glavine

Interior Design: Richard Stalzer

CONTENTS

Introduction

IN 1903, THE PITTSBURGH PIRATES had the best record in the National League and the Boston Pilgrims were tops in the American League. Boston owner Henry Killilea challenged Pittsburgh owner Barney Dreyfus to a postseason championship series. The two owners thought the series would keep up interest in baseball.

That is how the World Series began. Since then, the World Series has produced many outstanding performances by individual players. Yet it was not until 1955 that Major League Baseball decided to honor players with a World Series Most Valuable Player Award. Because of that, great players such as Babe Ruth, Ty Cobb, and Joe DiMaggio were never named World Series MVPs.

Sometimes the World Series MVP has been a Hall of Fame player, such as Bob Gibson or Reggie Jackson. At other times, the MVP has been a player with an average to below average major-league career, such as Don Larsen. One thing that all the MVPs have had in common was that they played their best when it mattered the most, when the championship of major-league baseball was on the line.

The ten players on our list helped their teams in different ways. Some won games with their hitting, some with their pitching, and others with their fielding or base running. We chose at least one player from every decade from the 1950s to the 1990s. That is why some outstanding World Series MVPs like Brooks Robinson (1970) and Lew Burdette (1957) are not on the list.

A lot of reading and statistics searching produced a list of five pitchers and five position players. None of the pitchers had a World Series ERA above 2.00. Only one of the batters (Reggie Jackson) had a World Series batting average under .380.

For the players picked, the question that had to be considered was: "Would their team have won the World Series if they had not played?" Eight out of ten times, our answer was probably not. Johnny Bench (1976) and Scott Brosius (1998) richly deserved their World Series MVP Awards, but their teams won the World Series in four straight games.

Three of the picks (Sandy Koufax, Bob Gibson, and Reggie Jackson) were two-time World Series MVPs. For them, the focus is on their most outstanding World Series.

Everyone may not agree with all ten of *our* choices, but we think you will agree that all ten deserved to be the MVPs of the World Series they starred in.

WORLD SERIES STATISTICS

Hitter	YRS	G	AB	R	H	HR	RBI	SB	AVG
JOHNNY BENCH	1976	4	15	4	8	2	6	0	.533
SCOTT BROSIUS	1998	4	17	3	8	2	6	0	.471
ROBERTO CLEMENTE	1971	7	29	3	12	2	4	0	.414
REGGIE JACKSON	1973, 1977	13	49	13	18	6	14	0	.367
MIKE SCHMIDT	1980	6	21	6	8	2	7	0	.381
Pitcher	YRS	G	W	L	ERA	SV	IP	K	SH
BOB GIBSON	1964, 1967	6	5	1	2.00	0	54	57	1
TOM GLAVINE	1995	2	2	0	1.29	0	14	11	0
OREL HERSHISER	1988	2	2	0	1.00	0	18	17	1
SANDY KOUFAX	1963, 1965	5	4	1	0.86	0	42	52	2
DON LARSEN	1956	2	1	0	0.00	0	10.2	7	1

Statistics for all players only include the year(s) that each won the World Series MVP award.

YRS=World Series MVP years	G=Games	AB=At-Bats	R=Runs H=Hits
RBI=Run(s) Batted In	HR=Home Runs	SB=Stolen Bases	AVG=Batting Average
ERA=Earned Run Average	W=Wins	L=Losses	SV=Saves
IP=Innings Pitched	K=Strikeouts	SH=Shutouts	

JOHNNY BENCH

THE 1976 SEASON HAD BEEN AN OFF YEAR for Cincinnati Reds catcher Johnny Bench. After averaging 33 home runs and 113 RBIs a season from 1970 to 1975, Bench slumped to hitting 16 home runs and 74 RBIs. Although he batted .333 in the National League Championship Series (NLCS), there was some talk that Johnny Bench was not the hitter that he used to be.

That talk ended after the fourth and final game of the World Series. The Reds backstop led a four-game sweep of the Yankees. After hitting a pair of home runs and recording 5 RBIs in Game 4, Bench finished the series with a .533 batting average, 4 extra-base hits, and 6 RBIs. He also showed baseball fans that he was one of the greatest defensive catchers in baseball history.

The New York Yankees had been a base-stealing team during their drive to the World Series. They had led the American League East, with 163 stolen bases in 159 games. In the American League Championship Series (ALCS) against Kansas City, they stole 4 bases in five games. Johnny Bench put a stop to that by holding them to one stolen base in three attempts. He also went through the Series without making an error or allowing a passed ball. It was Bench's hitting, though, that made him the popular choice for World Series MVP.

In Game 1, a single and a RBI triple in three at-bats helped to give the Reds an easy 5–1 win. Bench followed that with a double and single in Game 2. Game 3 was Bench's third straight two-hit game. It was also the only

Compared to his previous seasons, Cincinnati Reds catcher Johnny Bench had an off year in 1976. He got hot in the postseason, hitting .533 in the World Series.

JOHNNY BENCH

game in the Series where he did not score a run or have an extra-base hit. Even without that, the Reds won, 6–2.

As Game 4 approached, there was no more talk about Johnny Bench's lack of hitting. Now the talk was about a four-game sweep, which would make the Cincinnati Reds the first National League team in fifty-four years to win back-to-back World Series titles.

In Game 4, the Yankees took an early 1–0 lead. The score was tied 1–1 in the fourth inning when Bench came to bat with one man on base. Yankees starter Ed Figueroa had been New York's winningest pitcher that year, but Bench burned him for a two-run homer. The Reds went up, 3–1.

With one out in the ninth, the Reds were leading, 3–2. This time Bench had to face Dick Tidrow, who had been New York's best right-handed reliever. With runners on first and second, Bench was just hoping that he could drive in an insurance run.

"I just want to get one run in," Bench recalled. "I swing and again I can feel the whole thing. Up, up and gone. Three runs, we're up 6–2, and in for good. The thrill is indescribable."[1]

After feeling as if he had not done nearly enough during the regular season, Johnny Bench was delighted to help his team win its second straight World Series. "You can't believe what a relief it is for me to do something for this club," Bench said.[2]

After 1980, the wear and tear of catching made Johnny Bench move to playing first and third base. When he retired in 1983, he had career totals of 389 home runs, 1,376 RBIs, and 10 Gold Glove Awards for his fielding. In 1999, Bench was honored by the Society for American Baseball Research. Their members named him as the starting catcher on baseball's All-Century team.

Scott Brosius

Born: August 15, 1966, Hillsboro, Oregon.

High School: Rex Putnam High School, Milwaukie, Oregon.

College: Linfield College.

Pro: Oakland A's, 1991–1997; New York Yankees, 1998– .

Records: Shares World Series record for most home runs in consecutive innings.

Honors: World Series MVP, 1998; selected to the American League All-Star team, 1998.

Following through with his swing, Scott Brosius checks the distance of his shot. Brosius hit two home runs in Game 3 of the 1998 World Series on his way to the series MVP Award.

Internet Address

http://www.majorleaguebaseball.com/u/baseball/mlb/players/player_7466.htm

ROBERTO CLEMENTE

In the 1971 World Series, outfielder Roberto Clemente led the Pittsburgh Pirates comeback against the Baltimore Orioles after being down two games to none.

ROBERTO CLEMENTE

DURING THE 1971 WORLD SERIES, Roberto Clemente explained why the Series meant so much to him. "I'm thirty-seven and may not play in another Series," Clemente said. "Money means nothing to me, but I love competition—to me to compete is to compare, and that's everything."[1]

Although 1971 was Clemente's seventeenth season in the majors, it would be just his second and last World Series. In 1960, he had batted .310 in seven games to help the Pirates defeat the heavily favored New York Yankees. Yet the MVP went to a player on the losing team. New York second baseman Bobby Richardson got the award after setting a World Series record by driving in 12 runs.

In 1971, as in 1960, the Pirates were decided underdogs. The Baltimore Orioles entered the Series with a fourteen-game winning streak. The Orioles' pitching staff had four twenty-game winners and had led the American League in complete games (71) and team ERA (3.00).

Still, the Pirates had a bit of an edge in hitting. Pittsburgh had led the National League in team batting average (.274), doubles, and extra-base hits.

Even though Clemente had 4 hits in the first two games, the Orioles won, 5–3 and 11–3. That stretched their winning streak to 16 games, and many fans felt that the Series was all but over.

Then, in Game 3, Clemente helped break Baltimore's winning streak by running hard. In the seventh inning, he topped the ball and hit an easy grounder to pitcher Mike Cuellar. Cuellar was ready to make a routine throw to first until he saw Clemente sprinting to first base. The surprised pitcher made a bad throw. After that mistake, Cuellar walked Willie Stargell on four pitches. Before Cuellar could settle down, Bob Robertson tagged him for a three-run homer. Pittsburgh won Game 3, 5–1.

In Games 4 and 5, Clemente belted out four more hits, giving him 9 hits for the Series. Clemente was batting .429, and the Pirates had unexpectedly won 3 straight games. Orioles third baseman Brooks Robinson, who had been the World Series MVP in 1970, noted Clemente's performance by saying: "I thought he was great, but now that I've seen more of him, he's even greater than I thought."[2]

Baltimore extended the Series with a 3–2, ten-inning win in Game 6. In that game, Clemente did just about every-thing one player could do for his team. On the bases, his daring running stretched a double into a triple. He also homered. Defensively, he kept the winning run from scor-ing in the ninth inning by making a sensational throw from right field.

Roberto Clemente's solo home run in Game 7 ended up being the margin of victory for the Pirates. Pittsburgh won, 2–1, and Clemente took MVP honors for having 12 hits and batting .414.

Sadly, Game 7 would mark the end of Clemente's World Series career. In December 1972, an earthquake ravaged the country of Nicaragua, in Central America. Clemente inter-rupted his off-season break to raise money and relief supplies for the people there. On December 31, 1972, Clemente died aboard a plane that was delivering supplies to the earthquake victims. The plane crashed off the coast of Puerto Rico, and no survivors were found.

ROBERTO CLEMENTE

BORN: August 18, 1934, Carolina, Puerto Rico.

DIED: December 31, 1972, San Juan, Puerto Rico.

HIGH SCHOOL: Julio C. Vizcarrondo High School, Carolina, Puerto Rico.

PRO: Pittsburgh Pirates, 1955–1972.

HONORS: National League MVP, 1966; World Series MVP, 1971; elected to National Baseball Hall of Fame, 1973; only second baseball player ever to be pictured on a US postage stamp; selected to All-Star team, 1960–1967, 1969–1972.

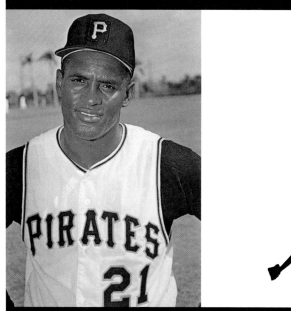

Clemente earned the 1971 World Series MVP with his hitting, fielding, and base-running abilities.

Internet Address

http://baseballhalloffame.org/hofers_and_honorees/hofer_bios/
clemente_roberto.htm

BOB GIBSON

St. Louis Cardinals pitcher Bob Gibson completes the pitching windup that allowed him to set many World Series records and win two series MVP awards.

WHEN RED SCHOENDIENST was Bob Gibson's manager at St. Louis, he summed up Gibson's pitching skills: "To put it simply," Schoendienst said, "he was just hard to beat."[1]

That was especially true in World Series competition. While pitching in three World Series, Gibson won two MVP awards (1964 and 1967) and 7 games in a row. He set World Series records for most consecutive complete games (8) and most strikeouts in one game (17).

As a child, Bob Gibson was sickly and skinny. He overcame a variety of childhood illnesses including asthma, hay fever, and a rheumatic heart. He turned to baseball and basketball because he was considered too frail to play high school football.

After signing with the Cardinals in 1957, Gibson continued to be a two-sport athlete. He played for the Harlem Globetrotters for one winter before devoting himself entirely to baseball. Gibson made his major-league debut in 1959, and by the mid-1960s, he was one of baseball's best pitchers.

In 1967, Gibson was having one of his best seasons. At midseason, he was 10–6 with a 2.44 ERA, but on July 16, he broke his right ankle after being hit by a line drive. He did not pitch again until September 4. In the last three weeks of the season, Gibson won 3 more games. He seemed to be fully recovered.

The Boston Red Sox had won the American League pennant while leading the league in runs, doubles, home runs, and team batting average. The St. Louis Cardinals would need a strong Series from Gibson to beat such a good hitting club.

Schoendienst picked Gibson to pitch Game 1. Gibson opened the Series with a 6-hit, 1-walk, complete game win. He struck out 10 and blanked the Red Sox for eight of nine innings. St. Louis won, 2–1.

St. Louis split the next two games before Gibson started Game 4. Another win would give them a commanding three-games-to-one lead.

Gibson turned in another outstanding performance. He blanked Boston, 6–0, while holding them to 5 hits. Gibson gave up one walk and struck out 6. In eighteen innings, he held the Red Sox to one earned run and 11 hits. His ratio of strikeouts (16) to walks (2) was an impressive eight to one.

Boston rallied to win the next two games. Gibson had been the winning pitcher in Game 7 of the 1964 World Series. Now his team needed him to win another Game 7.

"I loved the World Series," Gibson said. "I loved the competition, the challenge of playing the best the other league had to offer for the honor of being the best of the best. I loved the fact that the world championship would be decided when and only when I let go of the ball. . . ."[2]

For the third time in the Series, Bob Gibson pitched a complete game win. Along with holding Boston to three hits, Gibson added 10 more strikeouts and hit a home run in a 7–2 finale. He finished the Series with a 3–0 record, an ERA of 1.00, and 14 hits allowed in 27 innings. That performance left no doubt that Bob Gibson deserved to be the MVP of the 1967 World Series.

One year later, St. Louis was back in the World Series. They lost the Series to the Detroit Tigers in seven games. Gibson was the winning pitcher in two of the Cardinals' three victories. In Game 1, he set a Series record with 17 strikeouts. In Game 4, Gibson added 10 more strikeouts and won his seventh consecutive World Series game.

BOB GIBSON

BORN: November 9, 1935, Omaha, Nebraska.

HIGH SCHOOL: Omaha Technical High School, Omaha, Nebraska.

COLLEGE: Creighton University.

PRO: St. Louis Cardinals, 1959–1975.

RECORDS: Holds major-league season record for lowest ERA in 300 or more innings, (1.12).

HONORS: National League MVP, 1968; National League Cy Young Award winner, 1968, 1970; World Series MVP, 1964, 1967; selected to All-Star team, 1962, 1965–1970, 1972; inducted into National Baseball Hall of Fame, 1981.

Gibson pitched three complete games in the 1967 World Series.

Internet Address

http://baseballhalloffame.org/hofers_and_honorees/hofer_bios/gibson_bob.htm

TOM GLAVINE

The Atlanta Braves got lucky when pitcher Tom Glavine chose to play baseball instead of hockey after high school. Glavine went 16–7 for the Braves during the 1995 regular season.

SOMETIMES WHAT A PLAYER DOES OFF the field makes fans forget everything that he has done to help his team win. That is what happened to Atlanta Braves pitcher Tom Glavine in 1995.

In 1994, a players' strike ended the season in August and caused the World Series to be canceled. Glavine had been one of the key members of the player's union. Many fans did not remember him favorably.

Glavine knew it would be important for him to have a good season after the strike, but helping his team was still more important to him than his popularity. "I will certainly try to get off to a good start," Glavine said during spring training, "but I'll try to do it to help my team. Not to please fans or get people off my back."[1]

He did both by winning 16 games with an ERA of 3.08. His pitching helped Atlanta run away with the National League's Eastern Division title. The Braves finished twenty-one games ahead of the runner-up New York Mets.

Even though he did not win a game in the Division Series or the NLCS, Glavine pitched two good games. In 14 innings, he allowed only 12 hits while walking 3. His post-season ERA before the World Series was an impressive 1.93.

The first game that Tom Glavine pitched in the 1995 World Series was a bit less than an MVP performance. Glavine was the winning pitcher in Game 2, but his pitching was only so-so. It took him 99 pitches to get through six innings while giving up 3 walks, 3 hits, and 2 earned runs. Many pitchers will take only 100 pitches to throw a complete game.

In the newspapers the next day, the game story was not about how Glavine had outpitched his Cleveland Indians opponent, Dennis Martinez. It was about how Javier Lopez's two-run homer in the bottom of the sixth allowed Glavine to leave the game with a 4–2 lead.

After watching the Indians win Game 5 of the Series, Glavine was worried about having to pitch in Game 6. Cleveland had just beaten Atlanta's ace, Greg Maddux. Glavine was concerned that the Cleveland hitters would be making adjustments after seeing him pitch in Game 2. He asked Maddux what to do.

"Just go out and pitch your game," Maddux said. "Don't change."[2] Glavine took Maddux's advice. He kept the Cleveland batters off balance by going with his changeup. Aiming his pitches at the low outside corner, Glavine made a good hitting team look bad. In eight scoreless innings, the only hit the Indians got was a bloop single by Tony Peña.

Atlanta fans were unhappy that Glavine did not pitch the ninth inning, but he knew that it was time to leave. "I got the outs, but I was getting away with a lot of mistakes," Glavine said. "It was obvious by then that my breaking pitch had lost its bite, my change-up lacked some movement and my fastball had slowed."[3]

Mark Wohlers iced the game and the Series for the Braves by retiring the side in the ninth. Wohlers had his second Series save, and Tom Glavine had his second Series win and the MVP award.

Glavine and the Atlanta Braves made five World Series appearances in the 1990s. Yet the Braves only won once. Even though they kept losing in the Series, Tom Glavine pitched well. His Series ERA has been under 2.00 three times. Despite a bad Series in 1999 (0–1, 5.40 ERA), Glavine still had a 2.31 ERA in eight World Series games.

Tom Glavine

BORN: March 25, 1966, Concord, Massachusetts.

HIGH SCHOOL: Billerica High School, Billerica, Massachusetts.

PRO: Atlanta Braves, 1987– .

HONORS: World Series MVP, 1995; National League Cy Young award
winner, 1991, 1998; selected to National League All-Star team,
1991–1993, 1996–1998, 2000.

Glavine shows off the World Series MVP trophy. He was the winning
pitcher in two of the four Braves victories in the 1995 World Series.

Internet Address
http://www.majorleaguebaseball.com/u/baseball/mlb/players/
player_7641.htm

OREL HERSHISER

OREL HERSHISER BECAME A MAJOR-LEAGUE star even though he was not a high school standout. He did not even make the high school varsity baseball team until his junior year. "I was always a step behind the people I competed against," Hershiser said. "I usually wasn't even the best player on my team."[1]

When the Los Angeles Dodgers selected him in the seventeenth round of the June 1979 draft, Hershiser was not considered an outstanding prospect. Success came slowly. He played five seasons in the minors before making it to the major leagues.

Then, in 1988, Orel Hershiser became the most dominant pitcher in baseball. Hershiser put the Dodgers into postseason play by hurling a major-league record 59 consecutive scoreless innings. He finished with a record of 23–8.

Still, he knew his records would not mean much if the Dodgers did not win it all. To get to the World Series they would have to beat the New York Mets, who had beaten them 10 times in eleven regular season games. He helped the underdog Dodgers get there by winning one game and saving another in the National League Championship Series. His 1.10 ERA and 15 strikeouts in the NLCS earned him the first of two postseason MVP awards.

Going into the World Series, the American League champion Oakland A's were favored to beat the Dodgers. The home-run-hitting heroics of Mark McGwire and Jose Canseco had led them to 104 regular-season wins and a four-game sweep of the Boston Red Sox in the ALCS.

OREL HERSHISER

Los Angeles Dodgers pitcher Orel Hershiser had finished the 1988 season with 59 consecutive scoreless innings to set a major-league record.

The Dodgers, inspired by a dramatic home run by the injured Kirk Gibson, surprised the A's with a victory in Game 1. Los Angeles then took a 2–0 series lead behind Hershiser's masterful pitching in Game 2. Hershiser led the Dodgers to a 6–0 win by holding the slugging A's to only 3 hits while getting 8 strikeouts. He also helped the Dodgers with his hitting by stroking a single and two doubles in three at-bats.

"I may have pitched better games, though allowing only three hits and walking just two made it one of my best," Hershiser said. "But putting the offense and pitching together, I'd have to say it was the game of a lifetime. I love to hit, but I have to credit a little luck when I go three-for-three."[2]

The Dodgers clinched the surprisingly short series when Hershiser won Game 5. It was his second complete game win of the Series. This time he held Oakland to 7 base hits and 2 earned runs while striking out 9. He completed a superb series with 17 strikeouts in 18 innings and an ERA of 1.00.

After the Series, Dodgers pitching coach Ron Perranoski talked about Hershiser's season of excellence by comparing one sport to another.

"It takes a pure athlete coordinated as he is to maintain that kind of groove for so long," Perranoski said. "It would be like a bowler rolling 300 games every day for six weeks."[3]

Throughout the 1990s, Hershiser continued to enjoy postseason success. With the Cleveland Indians in 1995, Hershiser was the MVP of the ALCS. In the 1997 ALCS, Hershiser pitched 7 shutout innings for Cleveland. In 1999, he hurled 7 more scoreless innings for the New York Mets in the Division Series and NLCS.

OREL HERSHISER

BORN: September 16, 1958, Buffalo, New York.

HIGH SCHOOL: Cherry Hill East High School, Cherry Hill, New Jersey.

COLLEGE: Bowling Green State University.

PRO: Los Angeles Dodgers, 1983–1994, 2000; Cleveland Indians, 1995–1997; San Francisco Giants, 1998; New York Mets, 1999.

RECORDS: Holds major-league record for most consecutive scoreless innings, 59.

HONORS: World Series MVP, 1988; NL Championship Series MVP, 1988; AL Championship Series MVP, 1995; *Sporting News* Major League Player of the Year, 1988; NL Gold Glove Award winner, 1988; NL Cy Young Award winner, 1988; selected to National League All-Star team, 1987–1989.

Hershiser was named 1988 World Series MVP after striking out 17 hitters in 18 innings.

Internet Address
http://www.majorleaguebaseball.com/u/baseball/mlb/players/player_7714.htm

REGGIE JACKSON

REGGIE JACKSON HAD BEEN a World Series MVP once before (1973), but after his performance in the 1977 American League Championship Series, it looked unlikely that he would become a two-time winner. In the ALCS against Kansas City, Jackson batted a puny .125 with only one RBI and 2 singles in five games.

Early in the World Series against the Los Angeles Dodgers, Jackson's postseason batting slump continued. After three games, Jackson had 2 singles in 9 at-bats. The Yankees' cleanup hitter was batting .222 with 4 strikeouts and one RBI.

Jackson then turned it around by hitting home runs in Games 4 and 5. That was impressive, and it helped the Yankees take a three-games-to-two lead in the Series, but the best was yet to come.

When he took batting practice before Game 6, Jackson felt that he was going to have a great game. He was hitting pitches out of the park without even swinging hard. "I hit maybe forty balls during my time in the cage," Jackson recalled. "I must have hit twenty into the seats. Upper deck. Bullpen. . . . The baseball looked like a volleyball to me."[1]

In his first at-bat, Jackson did not need to swing. He looked at four straight pitches out of the strike zone. His next time up, he was through waiting. He hit the first pitch.

Dodgers pitcher Burt Hooton tried to get a fastball up and in. The pitch was up, but it was not in far enough. Jackson hit that mistake for a line drive home run into the right-field seats.

The fans look on in excitement as Reggie Jackson blasts another deep drive.

REGGIE JACKSON

One inning later, Elias Sosa was pitching for Los Angeles. Once again, Jackson swung at the first pitch. This offering was also out over the plate. It also ended up in the right-field seats.

"It was the hardest ball I hit all night," Jackson said. "A screaming line drive into right."[2]

Going back to Game 5, Reggie Jackson now had 3 consecutive home runs on three consecutive swings. Was he about to make World Series history? No one had ever hit 4 home runs in four consecutive swings. Only the legendary Babe Ruth had hit 3 home runs in a World Series game.

This time veteran knuckleball pitcher Charlie Hough would try to get Jackson out. A knuckleball is a very tricky pitch to hit. After seeing fastballs, would Reggie have the patience to wait on an off-speed pitch?

It took only one pitch for Jackson to answer that question. Hough's knuckler did not break as it should have. Jackson waited on the ball and met it with a perfectly timed, fully extended swing. The ball landed halfway up the center-field bleachers.

Reggie Jackson now held the record for most home runs (5) and runs scored (10) in a World Series. Teammate Thurman Munson gave him the nickname Mr. October. He also tied Babe Ruth's record of 3 home runs in a World Series game. The Yankees' newest World Series hero shied away from any comparisons with the Yankees' greatest slugger. "Babe Ruth was great, I'm just lucky," Jackson said.[3]

Before retiring in 1987, Jackson continued to excel in World Series competition. He batted .391 in the 1978 World Series and .333 in the 1981 fall classic. He set the record for the highest slugging percentage (.755) for twenty or more Series games. Thus, Reggie Jackson will always be known as Mr. October.

REGGIE JACKSON

BORN: May 18, 1946, Wyncote, Pennsylvania.

HIGH SCHOOL: Cheltenham High School, Cheltenham, Pennsylvania.

COLLEGE: Arizona State University.

PRO: Kansas City Athletics, 1967; Oakland Athletics, 1968–1975, 1987; Baltimore Orioles, 1976; New York Yankees, 1977–1981; California Angels, 1982–1986.

RECORDS: Holds World Series record for highest slugging percentage, .755; holds major-league record for most home runs in one World Series, 5.

HONORS: American League MVP, 1973; World Series MVP, 1973, 1977; had a candy bar named after him; selected to the All-Star team, 1969, 1971–1975, 1977–1984; elected to National Baseball Hall of Fame, 1993.

Jackson's Series MVP Award in 1977 was the second of his career. He also earned the honor for the Oakland A's in 1973.

Internet Address

http://baseballhalloffame.org/hofers_and_honorees/hofer_bios/ jackson_reggie.htm

SANDY KOUFAX

EVEN AFTER HE SIGNED A PRO CONTRACT with the Brooklyn Dodgers in 1955, Sandy Koufax did not think that baseball would be his career. At Lafayette High School in Brooklyn, New York, and at the University of Cincinnati, basketball had been his favorite sport. Signing a baseball contract for twenty-thousand dollars was just a way of making some quick money. "The last thing that entered my mind," Koufax said, "was becoming a professional athlete."[1]

Koufax's first World Series MVP Award had come in 1963. In Game 1, he set a new series record by striking out 15 batters in nine innings. Then, in Game 4, he completed the sweep of the defending champion Yankees. He registered 8 strikeouts in a 2–1 complete game win. It is hard to improve on a performance like that, but in 1965, many fans thought he was even more overpowering.

By 1965, Sandy Koufax was much more than just a professional athlete. He had become one of baseball's dominant pitchers. That season, he won his second Cy Young Award while leading the major leagues in wins (26), innings pitched (336), and strikeouts (382).

In spite of those glowing stats, there was still some concern about how the Dodgers pitching ace would do in the World Series. In spring training, the hard-throwing left-hander had been diagnosed with chronic arthritis in his left elbow. That condition would end Koufax's career one year later. Before the Series started, fans and sportwriters wondered how many pitches Koufax had left in his arthritic pitching arm.

The 1965 World Series tested the theory that good pitching beats good hitting. The American League champion

Los Angeles Dodgers pitcher Sandy Koufax won the
Series MVP Award twice in a three-year period.

SANDY KOUFAX

Minnesota Twins won 102 games while leading their league in team batting average (.254) and runs scored (774). Along with Koufax, Los Angeles had a 23-game winner in Don Drysdale, and its pitching staff led the majors in complete games (58), shutouts (23), and team ERA (2.81).

Koufax started Game 2. He would have started Game 1, but he refused to pitch on Yom Kippur, a Jewish holy day. He pitched well, going six innings and giving up 6 hits and 2 earned runs while striking out 9. However, Minnesota's Jim Kaat pitched an even better game, and the Twins won, 5–1. "Kaat pitched a better ball game than I did," Koufax said. "It was as simple as that."[2]

That was the last time that Koufax would be outpitched in the Series. In his next two starts, he was about as close to unhittable as a pitcher could be.

In Game 5, Koufax retired the first twelve batters while hurling a four-hit, complete-game shutout. He had 10 strikeouts and only one walk. Amazingly, Koufax said it was not one of his better games. "I had too many 2–0 counts today," Koufax said. "I had to keep coming back with my fastball when I should have thrown more curves."[3]

After the Dodgers lost Game 6, manager Walter Alston picked Koufax to start the Series-deciding seventh game. Koufax only had two days' rest, but once again he pitched superbly.

For the second time, Koufax blanked the hard-hitting Twins. This time he held Minnesota to 3 hits while getting 10 strikeouts. He also retired 14 of the last 15 batters. It was his second complete game of the Series and the 29th of the season.

Sandy Koufax finished the 1965 World Series with an ERA of 0.38. He allowed just 13 hits in twenty-four innings while racking up 29 strikeouts. Good pitching beat good hitting, and for the second time in three years, Sandy Koufax was the World Series MVP.

SANDY KOUFAX

BORN: December 30, 1935, Brooklyn, New York.

HIGH SCHOOL: Brooklyn Boys High School, Brooklyn, New York.

COLLEGE: University of Cincinnati.

PRO: Brooklyn Dodgers, 1955–1957; Los Angeles Dodgers, 1958–1966.

RECORDS: Holds the major-league record for most consecutive years leading the league in ERA, 5; youngest player ever elected to the National Baseball Hall of Fame.

HONORS: National League MVP, 1963; Cy Young Award winner, 1963, 1965–1966, World Series MVP, 1963, 1965; selected to the All-Star team, 1961–1966; named the Player of the Decade for the 1960s; elected to National Baseball Hall of Fame, 1972.

After losing Game 2 of the 1965 Series, Koufax came back to win Games 5 and 7.

Internet Address

http://baseballhalloffame.org/hofers_and_honorees/hofer_bios/koufax_sandy.htm

DON LARSEN

Yankees pitcher Don Larsen pitched poorly in Game 2 of the 1956 World Series, but came back to throw a perfect game in Game 6.

DON LARSEN

DON LARSEN IS REMEMBERED as the imperfect man who pitched the perfect game. When a pitcher retires 27 batters in nine innings without a batter getting on base, that is a perfect game. Don Larsen is the only pitcher to have a perfect game in the World Series.

When the New York Yankees acquired him from the Baltimore Orioles in 1955, Larsen had a career record of 10–33. In 1954, he had led the major leagues in losses (21) while winning only 3 games.

In Game 2 of the 1956 World Series, Larsen continued to perform like a below-average pitcher. The Yankees gave him an early 6–0 lead, but he was not able to go past the second inning. Although he did not allow any earned runs, Larsen gave up 4 runs, one hit, and 4 walks in one and two-thirds innings. The Yankees went on to lose to the Brooklyn Dodgers, 13–8. Larsen doubted that he would pitch in the Series again. "I figured that I had blown my chance," Larsen said. "I was sure I'd never get another chance to start in that Series."[1]

New York came back to win Games 3 and 4, to tie the series at two games apiece. Larsen was not expected to start Game 5, since there were two other well-rested starters available. But Yankees manager Casey Stengel still believed that Larsen was a much better pitcher than his record indicated.

"He can be one of baseball's great pitchers any time he puts his mind to it," Stengel said.[2]

On October 8, 1956, Don Larsen showed that Casey Stengel was right. Using a no-windup delivery, Larsen kept the Dodgers hitless with off-speed pitching and outstanding control. He was also helped by some timely defensive plays.

The first threat to the perfect game came in the second inning. Jackie Robinson's hard line drive jumped off the glove of Yankee third baseman Andy Carey. Luckily, the ball bounced into the glove of shortstop Gil McDougald, who fielded the ball in time to throw Robinson out.

In the fifth inning, Larsen survived two more close calls. Center fielder Mickey Mantle's sensational backhand catch robbed Gil Hodges of an extra-base hit. Brooklyn's next batter, Sandy Amoros, just missed a home run when his hard hit line drive curved foul at the last moment.

Hodges had another hit taken away in the eighth when Carey gloved a tricky low liner to the left of third base.

With three outs left, Larsen wondered whether he had the strength and composure to finish the game. "I was so weak in the ninth inning," Larsen said. "I thought I was going to faint."[3]

Larsen got leadoff hitter Carl Furillo to fly out to deep right field. Then he retired catcher Roy Campanella on a grounder to second. With one out left, the Dodgers went to their bench for a pinch hitter.

Brooklyn manager Walter Alston chose Dale Mitchell. Mitchell had a well-deserved reputation for being a contact hitter who was a tough out. He had batted .292 for Brooklyn that season.

On a 2–2 count, Larsen put a fastball over the outside corner for a called strike three. Mitchell started to swing before pulling his bat back. Larsen had his perfect game.

Don Larsen went on to enjoy further World Series success. He won Series games in 1957, 1958, and 1962. Altogether he pitched in ten World Series games, going 4–2 with a 2.75 ERA. He did not fare nearly as well during the regular season. Larsen retired after the 1967 season with a career record of 81–91 and a 3.78 ERA.

DON LARSEN

BORN: August 7, 1929, Michigan City, Indiana.

HIGH SCHOOL: Point Loma High School, San Diego, California.

PRO: St. Louis Browns, 1953; Baltimore Orioles, 1954, 1965; New York Yankees, 1955–1959; Kansas City Athletics, 1960–1961; Chicago White Sox, 1961; San Francisco Giants, 1962–1964; Houston Colt 45's, 1964; Houston Astros, 1965; Chicago Cubs, 1967.

RECORDS: Only pitcher in World Series history ever to throw a perfect game.

HONORS: World Series MVP, 1956.

Through the 1999 season, Larsen remained the only pitcher to have thrown a perfect game in World Series play.

Internet Address

http://www.sportingnews.com/archives/worldseries/1956.html

MIKE SCHMIDT

Prior to 1980, Phillies third baseman Mike Schmidt had not performed well in postseason play.

MIKE SCHMIDT

In **1980, Mike Schmidt Enjoyed** a two-MVP season. He won the regular-season MVP after he led the National League in home runs, RBI, slugging percentage, and total bases. He then led the Philadelphia Phillies to their first World Series championship.

Before the Series, Schmidt had experienced a pretty dismal record in recent postseason play. In the 1977 NLCS, he had only one hit in sixteen at-bats, for an anemic .063 average. The 1978 NLCS had not been much better. Schmidt had gone 3-for-15 for a lowly .200 average. The 1980 NLCS against the Houston Astros was more of the same. His 5 hits in twenty-four at-bats produced a .208 average. In his last 55 postseason at-bats, Mike Schmidt had only 9 hits, 3 RBIs, and no home runs.

When the Series against the Kansas City Royals began, Mike Schmidt must have felt he had something to prove. In an interview, Schmidt talked about the enormous pressure to play well. "You like to think that you can handle it," Schmidt said. "But for me it's hard. Heck, I'm not trying to fail. I'm concentrating every second that I'm on the field."[1]

In Game 1, Schmidt scored two runs to help give the Phillies a 7–6 win. In Game 2, his RBI-double helped the Phillies score 4 runs in the eighth inning to beat the Royals, 6–4. Although the Phillies lost Game 3, 4–3, Schmidt kept the score close by clubbing a solo home run. After Philadelphia lost Game 4, 5–3, Mike Schmidt enjoyed his finest game of the Series in Game 5.

Schmidt gave the Phillies an early 2–0 lead by swatting a Larry Gura changeup over the center-field wall. Philadelphia was trailing, 3–2, when Schmidt led off the ninth inning. He started a rally when Royals third baseman George Brett was not able to cleanly field his hard-hit ground ball. Schmidt was on with a single. Then he scored the tying run on Del Unser's double. Schmidt ended the game with 2 hits, 2 runs, and 2 RBIs in four at-bats, and the Phillies won, 4–3.

After five World Series games, Mike Schmidt was batting .438, and the Phillies were returning home to Veterans Stadium. They wanted to win the Series in their own park in front of their fans. Schmidt saw to it that they did.

In the bottom of the third inning, Schmidt came to bat with the bases loaded. He gave the Phillies a 2–0 lead by lining a single into right-center field. It was his eighth hit in six games. Philadelphia went on to win, 4–1, and Mike Schmidt ended the Series with a .381 batting average, 6 runs scored, and 7 RBIs.

After being named the World Series MVP, Schmidt suggested that the award should be shared with his teammates and be split twenty-five ways. He had wanted to win the Series, and he had hoped to win it. Yet he admitted that he had some doubtful moments. "I didn't count on winning," Schmidt said, "until after the last pitch. I'm still sort of in a coma."[2]

Mike Schmidt did not fare so well in his other World Series appearance. In the 1983 Series, Schmidt managed only one hit in twenty at-bats. The Phillies fell to the Baltimore Orioles in five games. That, however, was just a minor blemish on a stellar career. Baseball writers remembered his 548 career home runs. Mike Schmidt was elected to the Baseball Hall of Fame as soon as he was eligible.

Mike Schmidt

BORN: September 27, 1949, Dayton, Ohio.

HIGH SCHOOL: Fairview High School, Fairview Park, Ohio.

COLLEGE: Ohio University.

PRO: Philadelphia Phillies, 1972–1989.

RECORDS: Major-league record for most home runs by a third baseman, 509; shares major-league record for most home runs in one game, 4.

HONORS: National League MVP, 1980–1981, 1986; World Series MVP, 1980; selected to the All-Star team, 1974, 1976–1977, 1979–1984, 1986–1987, 1989; elected to the National Baseball Hall of Fame, 1995.

In the 1980 World Series, Schmidt silenced his critics by batting .381 on his way to being named MVP.

Internet Address

http://baseballhalloffame.org/hofers_and_honorees/hofer_bios/schmidt_mike.htm

Chapter Notes

Johnny Bench

1. Johnny Bench and William Brashler, *Catch You Later: The Autobiography of Johnny Bench* (New York: Harper & Row, 1979), p. 201.

2. Murray Chass, "Reds Triumph, 7–2, and Complete 4-Game Sweep of Yankees," *The New York Times*, October 22, 1976, p. A19.

Scott Brosius

1. Jack Curry, "Yankees Take $5 Million Hit to Deal Rogers," *The New York Times*, November 7, 1997, p. C3.

2. Buster Olney, "Brosius' Homers Put Yanks Within One Victory of a Title," *The New York Times*, October 21, 1998, p. A1.

3. Ibid.

Roberto Clemente

1. Kal Wagenheim, *Clemente!* (New York: Pocket Books, 1973), p. 188.

2. Ibid.

Bob Gibson

1. Ken Young, *Cy Young Award Winners* (New York: Walker & Company, 1994), p. 73.

2. Bob Gibson and Lonnie Wheeler, *Stranger to the Game* (New York: Viking, 1994), p. 141.

Tom Glavine

1. Steve Marantz, "The Two Sides of Tom Glavine," *The Sporting News*, May 1, 1995, p. S-5.

2. Tom Verducci, "Brave Hearts," *Sports Illustrated*, November 6, 1995, p. 28.

3. Tom Glavine with Nick Cafardo, *None but the Braves* (New York: HarperCollins, 1996), p. 3.

Orel Hershiser

1. Charles Moritz, ed., *Current Biography Yearbook 1990* (New York: H. W. Wilson, 1990), p. 298.

2. Orel Hershiser, with Jerry B. Jenkins, *Out of the Blue* (Brentwood, Tenn.: Wolgemuth & Hyatt, 1989), p. 193.

3. Peter Gammons, "A Case of Orel Surgery," *Sports Illustrated*, October 31, 1988, p. 37.

Reggie Jackson

1. Reggie Jackson, with Mike Lupica, *Reggie: The Autobiography* (New York: Villard Books, 1984), p. 209.

2. Ibid. p. 210.

3. Joseph Durso, "Yankees Take Series Jackson Equals Mark of 3 Homers in Game," *The New York Times*, October 19, 1977, p. B5.

Sandy Koufax

1. Charles Moritz, ed., *Current Biography Yearbook 1964* (New York: H. W. Wilson, 1964), p. 239.

2. Sandy Koufax with Ed Linn, *Koufax* (New York: Viking Press, 1966), p. 260.

3. Bill Becker, "Koufax's Complete Game His 28th of Year," *The New York Times*, October 12, 1965, p. 60.

Don Larsen

1. Glenn Dickey, *The History of the World Series Since 1903* (New York: Stein & Day, 1984), p. 191.

2. John Drebinger, "Larsen Beats Dodgers in Perfect Game," *The New York Times*, October 9, 1956, p. 1.

3. Joseph Reichler, *Baseball's Great Moments* (New York: Bonanza Books, 1985), p. 71.

Mike Schmidt

1. Bob Allen and Bill Gilbert, *The 500 Home Run Club* (Champaign, Ill.: Sports Publishing Inc., 1999), p. 237.

2. Joseph Durso, "Happy Phils Bind Old Wounds," *The New York Times*, October 23, 1980, sec. D, p. 19.

INDEX